A Safe Haven

Emma Zhang

BookLeaf
Publishing

India | USA | UK

A Safe Haven © 2022

Emma Zhang

Presentation by *BookLeaf Publishing*

Web: www.bookleafpub.com

E-mail: info@bookleafpub.com

ISBN: 9789357444361

First edition 2022

To every Asian who grew up in the West.
Regardless of where you are from, I dedicate
this to you.

ACKNOWLEDGEMENT

Thank you to my family for shaping me to be who I am today. To my mum, dad, brother, grandfather, and late grandmother. And thank you to every Asian out there who shares this journey together with me. With us.

PREFACE

When I first decided to publish my own book, all I knew was I wanted it to be something personal. Something that was close to me, but also something that others would be able to relate to and something that could help others. In the last four or so years, I've found myself continuously struggling to come to terms with who I am as an Australian of Chinese descent.

Am I Australian? Am I Chinese? Or can I be both or none at the same time? If you're an Australian Chinese who's also looking for an answer to that question, my honest answer is, I don't know. But what I do know is that my experiences aren't just my own and that most likely, every other Asian Australian, or Asian American, or Asian Canadian, or Asian who knows where, has also asked themselves the exact same question at some point in their lives. And all of us have at one point struggled to understand who and what we are.

That's why I decided to create this collection of poems keeping every Asian who grew up in the West in mind. The point of this book is not to show you that we all experienced the same things growing up, but rather to tell you that each of us have our own unique experiences that make us, us. That makes me who I am and makes you who you are. Whilst it may not answer the question of who you are for you, I hope this book can become a safe haven and source of comfort for every person struggling with their identity. Remember, you're not alone in this journey. We're all in this together.

Straight A's

Scratches of a pencil echo
as grey swirls form on sheets of A4
scattered across my desk.
Red marks flicker amongst the grey;
a memory from the past, and a signal of
what is to come.

But when A is for Average,
and B is for Bad,
and anything from C onwards is nothing but
worthless,
What other choice do I have?

I can only let the pencil continue its course
in contaminating those pure, white sheets,
watch it dye them grey,
and then red,
before they also end up scattered across my
desk.

Failure is not an option.
That choice isn't available.
So for either my sake, or theirs,
the scratches of my pencil
must, and will,
continue to
echo.

A

Smelly Lunches

3

Unscrewing the lid,
Aromatic herbs and spices
Our own smelly lunch.

Weekend Tutoring

Glimmers of warmth shine through the curtains;
my body curls under the soft comfort of the
blankets
content and satisfied, free from any burdens,
just relaxed, undisturbed and happy.

A cacophonic symphony sends a harsh
awakening.
I struggle to bury myself and mute my ears
but my journey to hell is just beginning.
Palm meets metal. I say goodbye to my day.

Screeches of seat legs and rustles of paper.
My steps drag as I enter a room of dark circles
slugged down from what's to come later.
I just hope I don't get called on.

The last light fizzles out.
The call of my name chills me through.
I hoped for an oasis in this drought.
I became everyone's oasis instead.

Internal cheers and blessings as they say
goodbye;
A restrained stampede as we race to freedom.
Walking out to meet fresh air and blue skies
We ignore the questions in our bag for another
week.

Bubble Tea

Beautiful black jewels
and tea's soothing bitterness
embraced in rich milk.

A Parent's Love: Bittersweet

There's no love that is not bittersweet.

Cinderella had to leave behind a glass slipper
to be found by her Prince.
Doraemon had to travel through his time
machine
to become Nobita's friend.
Hua Mulan had to fight for her country
to protect her father.
They had to travel to a foreign land with nothing
to give us everything.

The slipper in their hand will
give us a sore arm or leg
instead of delivering us a Prince.
Time travel will continue to exist only
in fairytales, drama, and movies
until someone finally makes it a reality.
But at least we won't have to fight
a country to protect them.
Because they've already done that.
For us.

Those slippers will continue to hurt;
The pressure to do well won't lessen;
The scolding for coming home late
will still make our ears bleed

But the fruit they bring into our room;
the weekly reminders they send us
to wear more clothes in Winter;
their glowing eyes and warm smiles
when we accomplish something new;
That's the sweet that comes after the bitter.

Bittersweet. That's what love is.
That's what their love is.

University Shenanigans

The true moment of pure rebellion
is when entering university finally settles in.
No more after school studying or curfews,
it's a whole new adventure. Our real debut.

Signing up for every club and society
The goal to attend each event becomes our top
priority.
Among the engineers, doctors, and lawyers in all
of us
studying is something that no longer kicks up a
fuss –

At least until mid-sems and finals anyway.
I'd take another HSC, IB or SAT exam over
those any day.
All-night crunches and breakdowns in a 24/7
library
The chances of being alive by the end is most
likely unlikely.

Yet we survive on our bright green cans of V
or iced long blacks or "americanos" or tea
and come out alive on the other side
battered and worn out from the crazy
rollercoaster ride.

But at least we're all in this adventure together
to sit through hours of lectures,
although whether or not we end up actually
listening to the professor
is not guaranteed until they call on you and you
feel the pressure.

Graduation

Warm hugs and proud smiles
Radiating happiness;
Finally complete.

Welcome Home

A foreign familiarity that ripples in the distance
like alienated memories of a forgotten
childhood;
The crescendo of chatters bubbling to the
surface
we take our first step out of the plane.

A flurry of chaotic, clumsy heavy lifters
Doctor-like scribbles in rectangular boxes
And empty eyes of machine-like blue uniformed
officers
Awaken a sleep-ridden nervousness and déjà vu.

Sudden time-skips and we become
the pollen that attracts the honeybees;
the magnet of attraction to not just some
but all the unknown faces that fill the room.

Uncomfortable interrogations meet plastered
smiles
As our grades, love life, insecurities and future
are laid out bare and stacked into several piles;
drying out the desert within our mouths even
further.

Soon, the overwhelming sensations of fatigue
and frustrations
Retreat like soothing waves bidding goodbye to
the soft sand
as the warm, comforting smiles form and leave
their fixations
to ensure our bowls never run empty.

It takes the passing of several days to become
more familiar
and reaching out for our somewhat rusty
language
to open up our hearts and minds to our families'
pillars.
But slowly, we embrace the mix of unfamiliar
feelings.

The feeling of not quite being home.
But also the feeling of arriving home.
Our not-quite-home home.
Welcome home.

Haggling

Walk up to the shop
Offer the lowest you got
Leave with goods and cash.

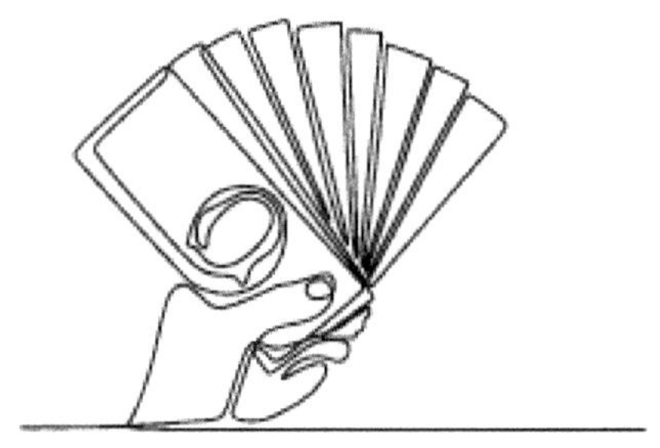

Yum Cha

Strings of steam swirl around
an endless sea of loud chatter and festivities
as bulky, metallic trolleys are
swiftly manoeuvred by ladies as strong as iron,
swivelling through the never-ending, narrow
maze of squares and circles.

Savoury, saliva-inducing smells
intermingle and flutter around
as pretty lazy Susan is spun over and over
by countless hungry fingers to share the
happiness
of what lays on her body.

A continuous clatter of plastic to ceramic
create a discordance of melodies that echo as
Siu mai, har gau and cheung fun,
or dim sum, dim sum and noodle;
make their way down the dark tunnel
that connect our mouths and stomachs.

Oh, and let's not forget the luscious,
juicy goodness of thin yellow,
fluffy white and fruity chunks that we call
mango pancake.

The soft plush of vermilion red and
warm coldness of bronze golds
create a bed of comfort when our food babies
arrive,
contrasting the quickly accelerating spitfire of
a Chinese rap battle between
mothers, aunties, grandmas, and mei neois
on just about every topic that came into
existence.

A buzz that we often tune out until a certain
topic decides to show its presence.
Also known as the paper with the stamps
Especially that piece of paper with the stamps.
The dreaded red stamps.

Excuse me while I just go to the toi-

Bilingual Struggles

Want to say something
But… zěn me shuō ne? I mean…
You know what I mean?

你好
Hello

Who am I?

When we were kids, we couldn't wait for
tomorrow.
Today was never enough. We wanted to grow
Older.
Smarter.
Faster.
We wanted everything the world had to give.
So we ran and ran
with no end in sight.
Without a care for anything else.
All we wanted was to grow up.

Years on, we start to lose our spark.
We start to slow down our steps…
Look back at photographs...
Turn back to yesterday.
Bring back nostalgic stories of when we were
Younger.
Brighter.
Happier.

Today becomes yesterday.
We turn back to yesterday.

But what about today?

What about now?
In this moment, what are we?

We see shadows of our past
and glimpses of our future;
but what do we see of now?

Who are we now?

Who are you?

Who am I?

Just Another Zhang

Descendant of the Yellow Emperor –
Bestowed a weighted offering
comprised of 'long' and 'bow'.
Our common trait dates back
to centuries ago. From the name of one,
now the name of MANY.

From a background of highest royalty
To the commonality of our every day,
The one characteristic that continues
to guide our ways extends from
the loaded power within the
origin of our name.

The courage to pick up the arrow
And settle its length upon the
string of the bow. The undivided focus
staring down at the moving target
ahead of us, fixated on hitting
that centre ring of ten.

The cunning manipulation of our hand
to adjust to the softest of breezes
or the hailing of a thunderstorm
may not land us at our destination;
but will carry us on a journey
far from where we are currently standing.

This weighted offering that we were presented
Without the option to refuse, only acceptance
May be a burden to some or a blessing to others:
Yet the unbridled power and recognition
Behind the bond of 'long' and 'bow'
Will continue to guide us towards the sun.

We might just be another Zhang
But all of us will continue to carry
the mind that created the origin of our name.

Where are you from?

When I buy a coffee to start the morning,
someone in line strikes a conversation.

"Where are you from?"
"I'm from Australia."

When I arrive at work a new colleague
walks up and introduces themselves.
Then comes the dreaded question.

"Where are you from?"
"I'm from Australia."
"No, but where are you really from?"
"I'm from Australia."

When I finish meeting with a client
and send them out,
they turn back to tell me something.

"By the way, your English is amazing! Where
are you from?"
"I'm from Australia."
"But you can't be, you don't look Australian."
"I'm from Australia."
"But surely you moved here from somewhere in
Asia?"

"I'm from Australia."

When I finally get home and nestle into the
comfort of my blankets,
I take a slow, steady, deep breath.
Ease my frustrations, and relax at the thought
that the day is finally over;
falling asleep a bit more at peace with myself.

"Where are you from?"
"I'm from Australia."

Real Conversations Between AB-somethings

When an ABC asks an ABK where they're
from:
"South Korea."
Uh…I meant which city in South Korea…

When an ABC meets another ABC:
"We have the same last name!"
This was between a Huang and a Wong.

When an ABK meets another ABK:
"You're a Kim? Which Kim are you?"
Apparently they're both Gyeongju Kims.

When two twenty-one-year-old ABJs hang out:
"Are you gonna keep your Japanese passport?"
Not sure…I'll decide by next year.

When a group of American Born Somethings
meet Australian Born Somethings:
"Why do you call McDonalds Maccas?"
Why not?

When the same group of AB somethings meet
again:
"So does yeah, nah mean yeah or nah?"
Yeah nah means nah. Like NAH-UH.

When the same group meets again:
"Why do you call water fountains bubblers?"
Because a water fountain is in the middle of a
park?

"What do you call your water fountains then?"
"They're also water fountains."
So you're telling me you call bubblers AND
water fountains water fountains???

Rice

The basic foundation that exists in our everyday;
round, soft grains that stick to each other
side by side - not too hard yet not a pile of mush.

The horrors that would come into existence
the day it ceases to exist ignites trembles and
shivers throughout the whole body.
What will become of our delicious mix
of bibimbap,
or freshly made nigiri?
How about our savoury nasi goreng,
elegant khao khai chiao
and fragrant pilafs?
Even just our steamy white rice, straight from
the rice cooker itself, ready to be served?
What will become of our habitual satisfaction
called rice?

Each grain comes from water tainted murky
with sweat, effort, love, and tears.
Of ploughing, planting, transplanting,
Harvesting, drying, hulling and milling…
Or a mix of any or all of the above…
Over and over and over.

If a man's humble request can cause an Emperor's
riches in rice to disappear from his kingdom,
our love and appreciation can be our tool
to save each grain we take.

Rice.
It's the foundation of our every day.
Don't waste it.

Asians on TV

As a child,
we danced along with five awesome people
who would sing and give us Hi-5's,
but we would only be drawn to
the one girl who looked like us on stage,
and ignore the other four
who were handsome and pretty
but did not represent us.

In our teenage years,
we watched four gorgeous girls
with light-coloured eyes and hair
shades of brown and blonde
rule the hierarchy we call school,
while those with black hair and
brown eyes all wore glasses and
had their nose in books at lunch time.

Now, in our twenties,
We learn that it is possible to
beat our mother-in-law at Mah-jong,
we can fight our father only
to end up with his ten-rings and
that hey, not every one of us
is actually perfect at speaking our
Asian language.

Subtle Asian Women

Stereotypical exotic young women
Submissive and timid without complaints
Neglected in favour of those who carry the
family's name
Not worth the effort, not worth the pain.

Old "traditions" edited and reinvented
Rebelling, fighting, driven by a force so strong
A desire to rewrite history into our own words;
Our own language, what we deserve.

Bonded by our roots, strengthened by the
Obstacles, breakdowns, suppressions,
Objections
Learning from each other, extending a hand
To crush and destroy Miss Internal Misogyny.

Sisters, daughters, mothers, mentors, friends,
partners,
A soft gold that fills in the gaps between broken
pieces;
Kintsugi. Each brush gently guides us closer to
being uniquely us. Our own version of us.

Within simmering dreams and rippling
insecurities,
We are the reflections from the burning sun;
Unbreakable glass from underneath the water.
Our one motivation to reach and break the
surface.

Beauty is YOU

A pretty V-shape and sharp jawline,
A thin, long nose with the highest bridge,
A single crease above the upper eyelid
Along with bright, dewy pale soft skin that is
Blemish free. Without a single fleck or line.

When the best shape is defined by S and D lines
or the twist of your arm to touch your navel.
An A4-sheet waist.
Or a visible block of
chocolate in the front and an equilateral
triangle in the back.
A height two-thirds your legs and a third of a
torso and face.
A white reflection
from beautiful clear skin.

Growing obsessions and addictions to
become the 'ideal' and the 'desired',
the perfect woman or man in a world of
chaotic misfits and unwanted individuality
that pushes and pulls you into a wilderness
of insecurities.

Hesitancy holds your hand when you meet
the homey comfort of a bowl of rice
or the greasy affair with a decadent burger.
A short celebration of staying true to your
partner
Before the inevitable appearance of a cheater
stutters and crashes down upon you.

In the pursuit of a non-existent reality;
A world of brilliance and perfection,
Of no mistakes, no fears, no judgement.
Lies an impossible quest of jealousy, hatred, and
betrayals.

Layered dome skirts are no longer our everyday.
Heels no longer represent esteemed aristocrats.
Pinks and blues are appreciated by everyone.
Trends of the present will soon become the past.

Cleopatra's charm was more than just her divine
looks.
Brahm's legacy lies in his symphonies and
sonatas.
Computer algorithms were not invented by
beauty.
Photo enhancement was not created for editing
selfies.

Dare yourself to take a step away from a dream
of flawless -
Open the door to authenticity, to self-healing, to
courage
Snap back from floating in a sea of confusion.
What kind of person do YOU want to be?

Be brave.
Take a step to YOU.
Beauty is not perfection.
Beauty is YOU.

Hóng Xiàn (Red Thread)

A fragile, thin invisible connection
blessed by the one and only Yuè Lǎo
linking two individuals together
at first, by their ankles, now
by the little finger on their hand.

Believed to survive the strongest of currents
And the hottest of flames, yet the
fear of losing our soulmate on
the other end of the line leads to
us grabbing a pair of scissors to
cut ourselves from a predestined fate.

Each individual is granted the
opportunity to meet their other half.
The yin to their yang. Whether your
string slowly wears down yet stays strong,
or frays and falls apart; comes down
to your choice of fear or love.

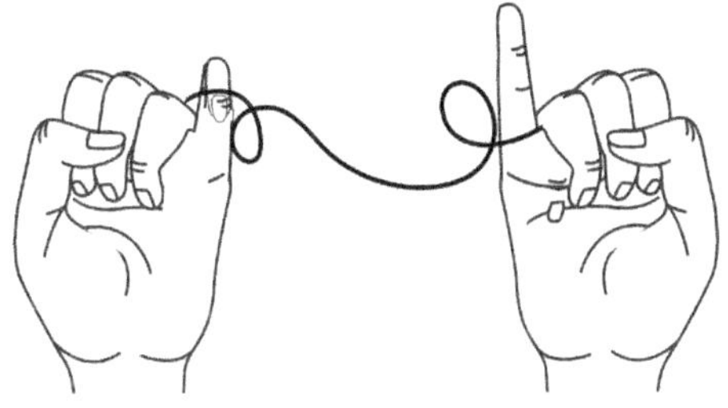

Our Tree

Made up of *four plus* billion individual leaves
each a separate shade of green.
Connected by two thousand three hundred twigs
of various thicknesses and lengths.
They meet forty-eight stronger branches
some closer to the ground, some closer to the
sky.
Supported by a steady, unwavering trunk
that holds it all together,
tied down to the ground by the
many roots that quietly extend beneath the
surface,
towards the unknowns of a hundred and
forty-seven.
Our tree.
Our community.

www.ingramcontent.com/pod-product-compliance
Lightning Source LLC
LaVergne TN
LVHW041233200726
843507LV00013B/2678